The

Hoffnung

Companion to Music

The

Companion to Music

IN ALPHABETICAL ORDER

By

Gerard Hoffnung

DOVER PUBLICATIONS, INC.
NEW YORK

This Dover edition, first published in 1971, is an
unabridged republication of the work originally
published by Dennis Dobson, London, in 1957.

International Standard Book Number: 0-486-22761-8
Library of Congress Catalog Card Number: 71-153740

Manufactured in the United States of America
Dover Publications, Inc.
180 Varick Street
New York, N.Y. 10014

*To Norman House
and its founder, Merfyn Turner,
the contents of this unworthy book
are affectionately dedicated*

Thanks are due to Messrs Bradbury, Agnew & Co Ltd, proprietors of Punch, and to Lieut-Col David McBain, Director of the Royal Military School of Music, Kneller Hall, for permission to include drawings which originally appeared in their publications.

The

Hoffnung

Companion to Music

A

Amateur

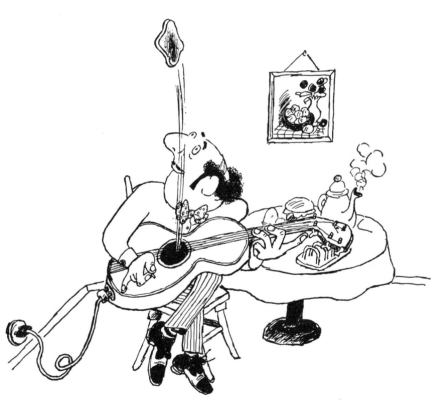

B

Bel Canto
(*see Hoffnung Music Festival*)

Bombardon
(*see illustration below*)

C

Concert Goers

Enthusiast

Prom fiend

Cougher

Time
beater

Le Sacre du Printemps

C

Critics

It is not dignified for
the music critic to applaud,
besides, he must not draw
attention to himself . . .

. . . except in the interval

The versatile reviewer who reports not only on music but, also, on crime, boxing and art

Reviewing in spirit

Double Bass
(*original version*)

E

Eine Kleine Nachtmusik
[Ger: A little night music]

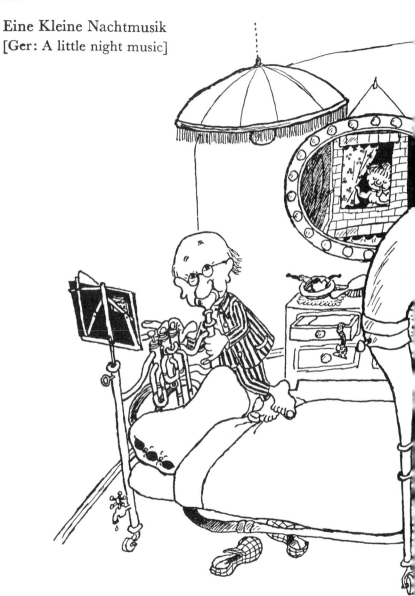

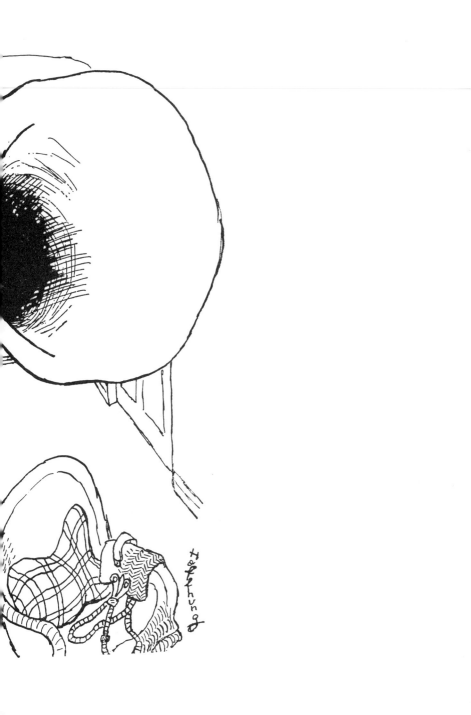

F

Fuoco
[It : Fire]
(*see Marche Militaire*)

G

Gebrauchsmusik
[Ger: Music for use]

(*see Eine Kleine Nachtmusik and Oxford Companion to Music*)

H

Horn making

I

Improvisation

J
Jazz

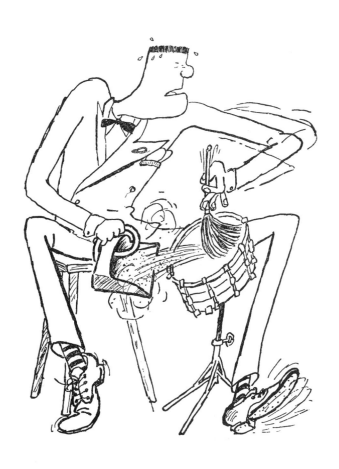

Jazz (*cont.*)

Tempo di Rock 'n Roll

K

Key signature

L

Lullaby

M

Marche Militaire

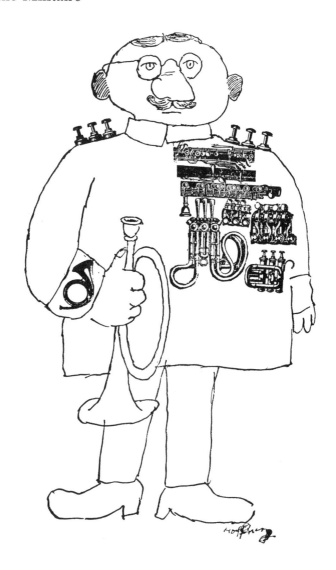

Marche Militaire (*cont.*)

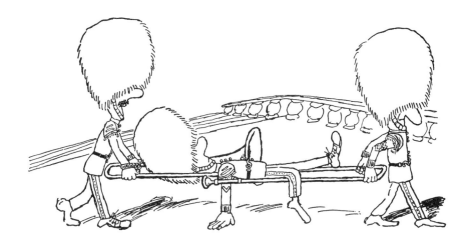

Marche Militaire (*cont.*)

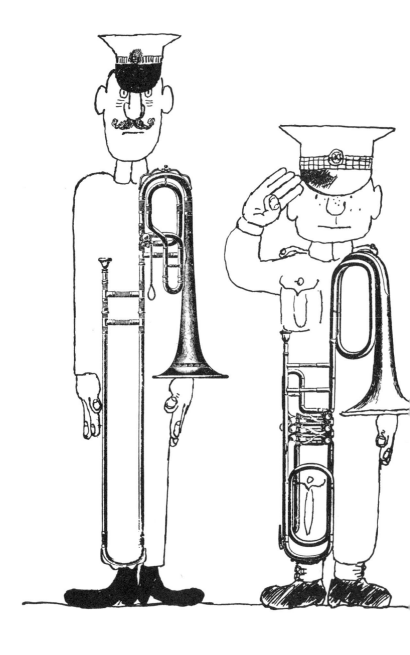

N

Nocturne
(*see Eine Kleine Nachtmusik*)

O

Oompah (*see author*)
Orchestral Thoughts
(*or Six Methods of Retaliation*)

OVER

Orchestral Thoughts (*cont.*)

P

Palm Court

Professional
(*see Amateur*)

Q
Quavitet
(*see Yongoneum*)

R

Rhythm
(*see Jazz*)

T

Telly

This medium is about **to establish**
a new bond of intimacy between the **musician**
and his audience

U

(*see Nancy Mitford*)

V

Volante
[It: In a flying manner]
(*see Orchestral Thoughts*)

W Well-tempered Clavier (*see Lullaby*)

X Xylophone (*see Zither*)

THE END